THE STORY OF SUGAR

First published in 2016 by Wayland
© Wayland 2016

Written by Alex Woolf
Cover illustration by Donough O'Malley

Designer: Balley Design Limited

A catalogue for this title is
available from the British Library

ISBN: 978075 029 6601

10 9 8 7 6 5 4 3 2 1

Wayland
An imprint of
Hachette Children's Books
Part of Hodder & Stoughton
Carmelite House
50 Victoria Embankment
London, EC4Y 0DZ

An Hachette UK Company
www.hachette.co.uk
www.hachettechildrens.co.uk

Printed in China

Picture credits: Picture credits: p4 © saurabhpbhoyar/Shutterstock; p5
© Aleksandr Makarenko/Shutterstock; p5 © Marcos Mesa Sam Wordley/
Shutterstock; p6 © Roxiller13/Shutterstock (t, l); p6 © Madlen/Shutterstock (m, l);
p6 © Filimages/Shutterstock (b, l); p6 © M. Unal Ozmen/Shutterstock (t, r); p6
© Leonid S. Shtandel/Shutterstock (m, r); p6 © stuart.ford/Shutterstock (b, r); p7
© Africa Studio/Shutterstock; p8 © PomInOz/Shutterstock; p9 © Geray Sweeney/
Corbis; p10 © Jim Gipe/AgStock Images/Corbis; p11 © Julian Stratenschulte/dpa/
Corbis; p12 © Milind Arvind Ketkar/Shutterstock; p13 © Universal History Archive/
UIG via Getty Images; p13 ©TopFoto; p14 © eans/Shutterstock; p15 © Image
Point Fr/Shutterstock; p16 © Madlen/Shutterstock; p17 © Stefano Bianchetti/
Corbis; p18–19 © The Granger Collection/TopFoto; p20 © Everett Historical/
Shutterstock; p21 ©Liszt Collection/TopFoto; p22 © Stocksnapper/Shutterstock;
p23 © Universal History Archive/Getty Images; p24 © Tarker/Corbis; p25 © Paul
Popper/Popperfoto/Getty Images; p26 © DEA PICTURE LIBRARY/De Agostini/
Getty Images; p27 © Edith S. Watson/National Geographic Creative/Corbis; p28
© PRImageFactory/Shutterstock; p29 © Maridav/Shutterstock. Background images
and other graphic elements courtesy of Shutterstock.com.

CONTENTS

WHAT IS SUGAR?

We sprinkle it on our cornflakes or stir it into our tea so they taste sweeter. It's an important ingredient in many of the foods we enjoy, such as cakes, jam, ice cream, soft drinks, chocolate and sweets. But what exactly *is* sugar? Where does it come from and why do we like it so much? In this book we'll explore the answers to these questions and delve into the sweet and sticky world of sugar.

MANY DIFFERENT KINDS

Sucrose is made up of two simpler sugars called *fructose* and *glucose*.

What we call sugar, scientists call *sucrose*, and sucrose is just one member of a whole family of sugars. Other sugars include *maltose* and *lactose*. All sugars belong to a group of nutrients called *carbohydrates*, which are our main source of energy. Carbohydrates also include *starchy* foods such as rice and potatoes. While sugars give us quick bursts of energy, starchy foods, which take longer to break down, give us energy over longer periods.

Sucrose is produced by plants through a process called 'photosynthesis' (see panel). All plants contain sucrose – which is why apples, carrots and almonds, for example, taste sweet. However, there are only two plants that store enough sucrose to make it worth growing them for their sugar. They are sugarcane and sugar beet.

HOW PHOTOSYNTHESIS WORKS

Plants soak up water from the soil through their roots, and take in the gas *carbon dioxide* through their leaves.

Leaves contain a green substance called 'chlorophyll'. The chlorophyll uses energy from the sun to combine carbon dioxide and water. This produces sucrose, which is stored in the plant. The result of this process is oxygen, which the plant releases into the atmosphere.

WHY DO WE LIKE SUGAR?

The human tongue can detect certain basic flavours, including salt, sour, bitter and sweet. Of these, we're drawn most of all to sweetness. Why is this? Humans belong to a class of animal called 'primates'. Other primates, such as monkeys and apes, live in forests and eat mainly fruit. They prefer ripe fruit over unripe fruit because it contains more sugar, which is a good source of energy. It's likely that humans did the same early in our evolution. We developed a taste for sweet fruit and this led to a taste for sweet things in general.

A CRYSTAL JEWEL

When seen under a microscope, a grain, or *crystal*, of sugar is like a jewel, it reflects light from its many sides.

Humans have always had a taste for sweet things. Today, there are more sugary foods available than ever.

HOW SUGAR IS USED

We usually think of sugar as just a sweetener, but it does lots of other things to food, too. For example, it can give texture and thickness to foods such as cakes and ice cream. It can also balance the sourness, bitterness or acidity of certain ingredients to make food more tasty.

DIFFERENT SUGARS

There are many different kinds of sugar and each is used in different ways. Here are some of the main ones:

Granulated sugar (granulated means 'formed into grains'): This is regular table sugar.

Brown sugar gets its colour from a black syrup called *molasses*, a natural leftover of the sugar-making process. The molasses is removed to make white sugar.

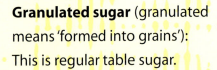

Caster sugar is fine-grained sugar used to make cakes. Its fineness allows it to blend smoothly with other ingredients to give food an even texture.

Icing sugar is very fine-grained sugar. Because of its powdery form, it dissolves quickly and is ideal for icing cakes and baked goods.

Sugar cubes are white or brown granulated sugars that have been lightly steamed and pressed into cubes.

Syrups and treacles: Syrups are made by dissolving sugar in water. Treacles are made by adding molasses to the mixture to give a richer, stronger flavour.

SUGAR GLASS

Have you ever seen an actor fall through a glass window in a movie and wondered how they don't hurt themselves? It may be because the glass was actually made from sugar! Sugar glass is made by dissolving sugar in water, then heating it to a high temperature. This makes it transparent and hard, but easily breakable, and it shatters just like real glass, so it's ideal for stunt work. But it must be used quickly, or it will start to soften.

GIVING FOOD TEXTURE

Sugar can add texture, as well as sweetness, to food. For example, syrup (dissolved sugar) is often used in recipes, not just because it's sweet, but because it's thick and sticky. This texture is important to the overall experience of certain foods. In fact, manufacturers of foods that use artificial sweeteners instead of sugar often add thickening agents such as starches or vegetable gums to replace the lost texture.

PRESERVING FOOD

Why can you keep jam for ages and it doesn't go off? It's all down to sugar. The sugar draws water out of the fruit in the jam, weakening the *microorganisms* that live in it and cause it to spoil. So how does sugar do that? The cells of all plants and animals, including fruit, are enclosed in a thin wall called a *membrane*, which water can flow through.

When a high concentration of sugar is placed outside a cell membrane, water molecules are drawn out of the cell. In jam, a sugar content of 65 per cent is needed to prevent spoilage. The natural sugar content of fruit is less than 65 per cent, so sugar must be added.

Sugar is a natural preservative that keeps foods like jam from going bad.

SUGARCANE

Sugarcane is a relative of ordinary grass. It grows up to 5 metres in height and is cultivated in tropical and semi-tropical parts of the world – places such as Brazil and India, where it's hot all year round with a heavy rainy season. Sugarcane is grown on large farms called plantations.

FARMING SUGARCANE

After the land is prepared by ploughing, short sections of cane called 'setts' are planted, and new shoots and roots grow from 'eyes' in the sett. It takes 11–18 months for the cane to produce enough sugar to be ready for harvesting. Traditionally, sugarcane was harvested by hand using large knives called machetes. Today, many plantations use machines. On average, a hectare produces 50 tonnes of sugarcane per year, yielding 7 tonnes of sugar.

Today, sugarcane is often harvested by machine. Machines can only be used where the land is flat.

RATOONING

Sugarcane can be harvested by chopping down the stems but leaving the roots in the ground so that the plant regrows. This process, called ratooning, causes the crop to mature more quickly and reduces the cost of preparing the field and planting. However, it leads to a smaller sugar crop, and it decreases with each crop cycle. About every three to ten years, the field must be ploughed and new setts planted.

EXTRACTION

Inside the hollow, bamboo-like stems of the cane is cane juice, which is rich in sucrose. After harvesting, the cane is taken to a sugar mill where it is crushed in roller mills to extract the cane juice. The juice is cleaned to remove unwanted ingredients, then the water is *evaporated* away to leave a thick syrup. The syrup is boiled again until sugar crystals grow. *Centrifuges* – machines that rotate liquids at high speeds – separate the crystals from the remaining liquid, which is known as molasses. The result is soft brown sugar that is ready for *export*, but still needs cleaning – or refining – further before it can be sold and eaten.

BAGASSE

The fibre from the crushed sugarcane, known as bagasse, is burned to provide power for the sugar mill. The burning bagasse heats boilers, creating high-pressure steam, which is passed through a *turbine* to generate electricity.

REFINING

Sugar is usually refined in the country where it will be consumed. Each stage of the refining process removes the unwanted parts of the sugar, known as impurities, and the colour to end up with pure white sugar. The stages are:

1 Affination: sugar is mixed with pure, concentrated syrup, then spun to separate the sugar crystals from the syrup. The crystals are then dissolved in water to make a purer syrup.

2 Carbonatation: lime and carbon dioxide are mixed into the purer syrup, causing chalk particles to form. The chalk particles trap or absorb any impurities and are then filtered out of the syrup.

3 Decolourisation: a form of carbon called granular activated carbon removes most of the colour, leaving a light-coloured syrup.

4 Boiling: the syrup is boiled until sugar crystals grow. The mixture is then centrifuged to separate out the crystals. The crystals – now pure white sugar – are dried, packed and stored ready for despatch.

SUGAR BEET

Sugar beet is a pale brown root crop that looks like a bit like a fat parsnip. It grows in temperate climates such as those found in Europe and North America. Sugar beet stores sucrose in its big, round root as a source of energy to get it through the winter. So beets are sown in spring and harvested in autumn or early winter when the amount of sugar they contain is at its highest.

BEET VERSUS CANE

The sugar content of beet is 13–18 per cent of the total weight, while in cane it is 10–15 per cent. However, both produce similar amounts of sugar. Cane mills tend to be more eco-friendly than beet factories because their energy is supplied by the *biofuel* bagasse (see page 9), whereas beet factories usually get their electricity by burning *fossil fuels*, which are more harmful to the environment.

A farmer with a freshly harvested sugar beet.

COSSETTES

When the beets are harvested, the top leaves are cut off and used as cattle feed or ploughed back into the land as a fertilizer. The beets are thoroughly washed to clean off any soil before being delivered to the factory. Here they are sliced into thin chips called cossettes. This increases their surface area, making it easier to extract the sugar.

DIFFUSING AND PRESSING

The cossettes are placed in a tank of hot water called a diffuser. The water, stirred by a rotating screw, becomes a stronger and stronger sugar solution, usually called juice. After diffusing in the hot water for about an hour, the cossettes are crushed in screw presses to extract any remaining juice. The pulp is turned into pellets for animal feed.

Sugar beets await processing at a factory in Germany.

CARBONATATION AND BOILING

The juice then undergoes carbonatation to remove any non-sugar impurities (see page 9). After that, it's placed in a huge pan (capable of holding around 60 tonnes of juice). In the pan, more water is boiled off the juice until conditions are right for sugar crystals to grow.

Once the crystals have grown, the mixture is centrifuged to separate out the crystals from the juice, now known as beet molasses. The resulting crystals are white and suitable for consumption. They're dried with hot air, then packed and stored ready for shipping.

BEET MOLASSES

This sweet, syruppy leftover product of the beet sugar-making process is usually turned into cattle food or sent to a *distillery* where it is used to make alcohol. Some of it is even used to help to save lives.

Molasses is added to the salt used for de-icing roads in North America. This lowers the freezing point of salt, which reduces the freezing point of water so roads don't freeze over as easily and are safer to drive on.

ANCIENT TIMES

The origins of sugar are not known for sure, but there is evidence that sugarcane was first grown on the island of New Guinea in the south-west Pacific from around 9000 BCE. People discovered that the stalks of the giant grass contained a sweet-tasting juice that could be consumed raw or used in the preparation of food. At religious ceremonies, New Guinean priests sipped sugar water from coconut shells.

SUGAR REACHES INDIA

From New Guinea, sugarcane cultivation gradually spread north from island to island until it reached the coast of India in around 1000 BCE. In the 4th century BCE, Indian cane growers worked out a process of making sugar crystals by evaporating cane juice. In about 325 BCE, a government official by the name of Kautilya wrote a book called *Arthashastra* in which he referred to five kinds of sugar, including *khanda*, from which we get the word *candy*.

At this plantation in India, hand-harvested sugarcane is loaded onto carts pulled by bullocks.

THE SECRET SPREADS

Knowledge of sugar spread to the West. The Persians discovered it in about 510 BCE, when their armies, led by Darius, invaded India. In 327 BCE, the Persian Empire was invaded by the Macedonian king, Alexander the Great, and sugar was introduced to the Greek world.

Sugar spread east to China by more peaceful means. In about 200 BCE, the Chinese emperor T'ai Tsung sent a mission to India to study how sugar was made. As Buddhism established itself in China in the first century CE, so did a love of sugar because Buddhism taught that sugar had healing properties.

Alexander the Great helped introduce sugar to the Greeks.

THE CLASSICAL WORLD

The ancient Greeks and Romans knew about sugar, but they continued to use honey as a sweetener, probably because it was more widely available. However, the Romans did occasionally *import* sugar for use as a medicine. The Greek naturalist and physician Dioscorides (c. 40–90 CE) described sugar as 'a kind of solidified honey called *saccharon* found in reeds in India … of a similar consistency to salt.'

Dioscorides recommended sugar as a cure for stomach, bladder and kidney pain.

HONEY WITHOUT BEES

The first reference to sugar in the West was made by Nearchus of Crete, an admiral in Alexander's army, in about 325 BCE. Until that time, Europeans had used honey to sweeten their food, so Nearchus described it as 'a reed in India [that] brings forth honey without the help of bees.' He goes on to describe sugar crystals as 'stones the colour of frankincense, sweeter than figs or honey.'

SUGAR AND OUR HEALTH

In a balanced, healthy diet, around half of our energy should come from carbohydrates – that's starches and sugars. The majority of this carbohydrate intake should come from starchy foods such as cereals, potatoes, pasta, rice and bread. The rest – around 10 per cent – should come from sugar. In other words, sugar should make up about 5 per cent of what we eat. That amounts to 24 g (six sugar cubes) a day for children aged seven to ten, and 30 g (seven sugar cubes) a day for adults.

TOO MUCH SUGAR

Most people consume too much sugar. We get sugar from foods that naturally contain it, such as fruit, fruit juice and honey, as well as from sweet foods that have had sugar added – cakes, biscuits, chocolate, fizzy drinks and sweets. Also, many of the non-sweet foods we buy contain sugar, including canned soup, salad dressing, tomato sauce and bread. On top of that, we often add granulated sugar or syrup to foods and drinks such as cereal, tea and pancakes. We're getting sugar from so many different sources, it can be quite difficult to limit how much we eat.

Sweets are delicious, but they have very high sugar content and should be consumed as an occasional treat, not every day.

14

OBESITY

We actually get enough sugar for our energy needs from fruit, honey and unsweetened fruit juices. Sugary foods should be no more than an occasional treat, and only consumed in small amounts. If we eat them too often, we consume more *calories* (units of energy) than we need. The excess energy is converted into body fat, causing us to gain weight. Being overweight or obese increases the risk of developing health conditions such as heart disease and *type 2 diabetes*.

A woman testing for diabetes by the finger prick method.

TOOTH DECAY

Eating too much sugar can also lead to tooth decay. *Bacteria* in our mouths use sugar to produce acid, which can form holes known as cavities. The longer sugary food is in contact with teeth the more damage it can cause. The sugars found naturally in fruit are contained within its structure so are unlikely to cause damage, but juicing or blending fruit releases the sugar, making it more harmful to teeth. The sugar in dried fruit tends to stick to teeth, so eating fresh fruit is better.

HEALING WOUNDS

For centuries, sugar has been used to help the healing of wounds. If granulated sugar is poured directly onto a cut or sore, it draws out the water, drying out the wound. Bacteria thrive in water, so this prevents infection and speeds up the healing process.

A CURE FOR HICCUPS

Hiccups are spasms in a muscle called the diaphragm. According to a traditional remedy, they can be cured by swallowing a spoonful of sugar. In one test, the method proved effective on 19 out of 20 patients. No one knows why.

THE MIDDLE AGES

It was thanks to the Muslim Arabs that sugar finally became an established crop in the Western world, replacing honey as people's preferred sweetener. As in ancient times, this came about through military conquest. In CE 642, when the Arabs invaded Persia, they discovered sugarcane and learned the secret of turning it into sugar.

ARAB SUGAR MAKERS

As the Arab armies spread through North Africa and Spain, they took sugarcane and sugar-making techniques with them. Sugarcane is a thirsty crop, and the Arabs were skilled at building *irrigation* systems to deliver water to the cane fields. They successfully grew sugarcane in Egypt, Syria, Cyprus, Rhodes, Tunisia, Morocco, Sicily and southern Spain.

Different grades of sugar were produced, ranging in colour and grain size. The Arabs even learned how to refine sugar to white crystals. In CE 990, to celebrate the end of the Muslim fast know as Ramadan, Egyptian sweet makers sculpted figures of trees, animals and castles out of white sugar.

MARZIPAN MOSQUE

Muslim rulers liked to flaunt their status by commissioning over-the-top sugar displays. One 15th-century caliph ordered the building of an entire mosque made from marzipan (a mixture of ground almonds and sugar). He later offered it to beggars who hungrily devoured its domes and minarets. Another ruler, Murad III (1546–1595), sultan of the Ottoman Empire, ordered his *sukker nakkasarli* (sugar artists) to create a procession of enormous sugar giraffes, elephants and lions.

CRUSADERS

Gradually, awareness of sugar spread throughout Europe. The first Britons to taste it were probably crusaders fighting against Arab Muslims in Syria in CE 1099. They came home full of tales of this delicious new 'spice'. When the crusaders invaded Sicily and Cyprus, they discovered cane fields and mills, and learned how to produce sugar for themselves. A small industry was born.

Sugar was transported in 'loaf' form: syrup was poured into conical ceramic moulds where it cooled and crystallized into a dark brown sugar loaf.

The cost of growing and transporting sugar was high, and it remained a luxury that few Europeans could afford. In 1264, it was recorded as an item in the kitchens of King Henry III of England. By 1319, it was selling for two shillings (about £50 today) for 0.45 kg. Sugar was so valuable that many people kept it inside locked cabinets.

In the Holy Land, crusaders met Arab traders carrying sugar, which they called 'sweet salt'.

SWEET MEDICINE

Sugar was valued by the Arabs not only for its sweetness but also for its apparent medicinal properties. From the 10th century, Islamic texts were recommending sugar as a means of masking the nasty taste of medicines or as a medicine in itself. Europeans were soon doing likewise. In the 12th century, the Italian philosopher and priest Thomas Aquinas wrote: 'Though they are nutritious in themselves, sugared spices are nonetheless not eaten [for] nourishment, but rather ease of digestion'.

SUGARCANE IN THE AMERICAS

In 1493, the explorer Christopher Columbus made his second voyage to the Americas – know as the *New World* – landing on the Caribbean island of Hispaniola. He carried with him some sugarcane to see how it would grow. The crop flourished in the fertile soil and hot, humid climate. This was a key moment in the history of sugar because, as Columbus reported to Queen Isabella of Spain, it grew faster here than it did anywhere in Africa, Europe or Asia.

BIRTH OF AN INDUSTRY

An industry was soon established. Over the following centuries, farmers from Spain, Portugal, Britain, France, Holland, Denmark and Sweden flocked to the New World, drawn there by the promise of making money from sugar. They cleared large areas of rainforest in the West Indies and South America to create huge sugarcane plantations. Sugar became known as 'white gold', and owning a sugar plantation was said to be like owning a gold mine.

At first the local population was employed to tend the crop, but many of them died from exhaustion through overwork, or from diseases introduced by western explorers, such as smallpox and measles. Slaves were brought in from Africa to labour on the sugar plantations.

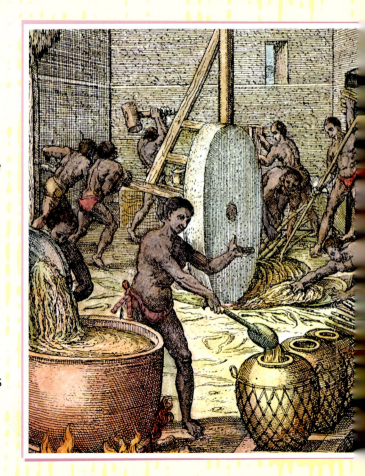

COMPETING NATIONS

Brazil, a Portuguese *colony*, dominated the sugar industry during its early history. By 1540, there were 2,800 cane sugar mills in Brazil and on its islands, churning out sugar. By 1612, Brazilian sugar production had reached 14,000 tonnes a year. As production increased, the price fell, boosting demand back in Europe. From the 1650s, sugar started to change from a luxury spice to a staple, first for the upper and middle classes, and later for the poor.

In the early 1700s, Brazil began facing serious competition from the French and British in the Caribbean. Unlike the Portuguese producers of sugar, they were helped by royal support. This made it easier for them to cope with the falling price of sugar due to the sudden rise in supply. They introduced new sugarcane products, including different types of sugar, syrups, rum and molasses. By 1750, the largest sugar producers in the world were French-controlled Saint-Dominique and British-controlled Jamaica.

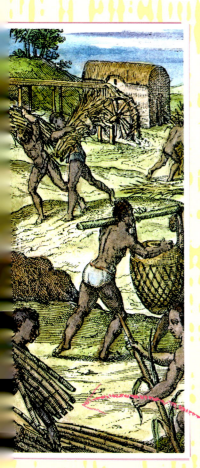

African slaves work on a sugar plantation in the West Indies.

THE FIRST PLANTATION

The very first sugarcane plantation in the New World was founded on the north coast of Jamaica in 1509. Eighty Spanish colonists were sent there by the Governor of the Indies, Diego Columbus, son of Christopher. The colonists planted sugarcane and forced the Taino – the native population – to work on it. They named their plantation Sevilla la Nueva. In 1515, the colony's second governor, Francesco de Garay, built a large, water-powered sugar mill there for extracting the cane juice, capable of producing 150 tonnes of sugar a year for export to Europe. The plantation did not last long, however: the site was abandoned in 1534. As for Jamaica's Taino, they were all but wiped out within 100 years, victims of European disease and exploitation.

SUGAR AND SLAVERY

The sugar planters soon realised they lacked sufficient manpower to plant and harvest the cane and process it into sugar. The first slave ships arrived in the early 1500s. Most of the slaves came from West Africa where the Portuguese had already established trading outposts. The slave trade continued for the next 300 years. In that time, more than 11 million Africans were shipped to the New World. Over half of them ended up on the sugar plantations.

The voyage took three to four months and the slaves were kept in appalling conditions.

TRADE TRIANGLE

A 'Trade Triangle' developed where slaves were sent from Africa to New World plantations, then the sugar they produced was sent to Europe, and the profits from the trade were then used to buy more slaves in Africa. While the sugar barons grew very wealthy, the slaves suffered. They first had to endure the journey across the Atlantic, known as the Middle Passage. Most of the way the slaves lay chained in rows on the floor or on shelves in the ship's smelly, filthy hold. Over the 300 years of the slave trade, at least two million slaves died during the Middle Passage, from disease, suicide or while trying to resist.

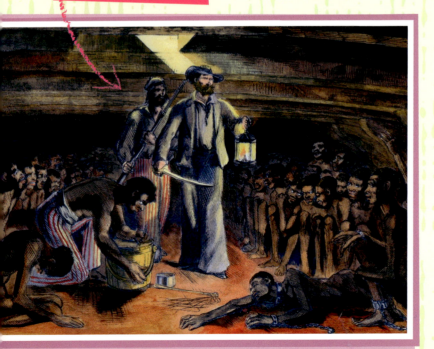

LIFE ON THE PLANTATIONS

On arrival in the Americas, slaves were sold to plantation owners at a public auction. They were then branded and issued with a new name. Life on the plantation was extremely harsh. Slaves were forced to work for up to 18 hours a day in the fields and pressing houses. There were no days off. Beatings were a common punishment for disobedience. If they failed to work hard enough, they might be put in neck collars or leg irons. Those who resisted through violence or by trying to escape were put to death.

Life expectancy was short – just seven to nine years on many plantations.

RESISTANCE

No matter what punishments were handed out, slaves often rebelled. Acts of resistance included deliberately working slowly, pretending to be ill, 'accidentally' breaking tools, starting fires or running away. Full-scale uprisings were common, especially towards the end of the 18th century, and the British were forced to keep a large military force on their Caribbean sugar islands because of the constant threat of a slave revolt. In 1783, a movement began in Britain to abolish the slave trade, and this was finally achieved in 1807.

THE REAL PRICE OF SUGAR

Many Europeans were aware of the human cost of their love affair with sugar. In his novel *Candide* (1759), the philosopher Voltaire writes of a slave who is missing both a hand and a leg. The slave explains: 'When we work in the sugar mills and we catch our finger in the millstone, they cut off our hand; when we try to run away, they cut off a leg; both things have happened to me. It is at this price that you eat sugar in Europe.'

SUGAR BEET IN EUROPE

In 1600, a French scientist named Olivier Serres noticed that 'The beet-root, when being boiled, yields a juice similar to syrup of sugar.' Beet had been grown for food and animal food since ancient times, but this was the first recorded instance of someone recognising its potential as a source of sugar. However, it would take a further two centuries before that potential was realised and the farming of sugar beet began.

SCIENTIFIC DISCOVERY

In 1747, Andreas Marggraf, a German chemist, managed to extract sugar crystals from beet juice. His discovery received little attention and Marggraf soon lost interest. However, his student, Franz Carl Achard, decided to continue with the research. He discovered a variety of beet that was very rich in sugar, and by 1786 he had developed a cheap method of extracting it. In 1802, Achard established the first beet sugar factory.

NAPOLEON AND THE BEET INDUSTRY

The first beet sugar factory was opened during the Napoleonic Wars, when the French Empire, led by Napoleon I, was fighting a group of European countries, including Britain. In 1806, the British navy blocked French ports and cut off France from its colonies, and sugar. As a result, the price of cane sugar rocketed.

Napoleon, who had heard about Achard's work, ordered sugar beet to be grown to replace cane sugar. Jean-Baptise Quéruel developed a way of producing beet sugar on an industrial scale.

Napoleon played a key role in developing the sugar beet industry.

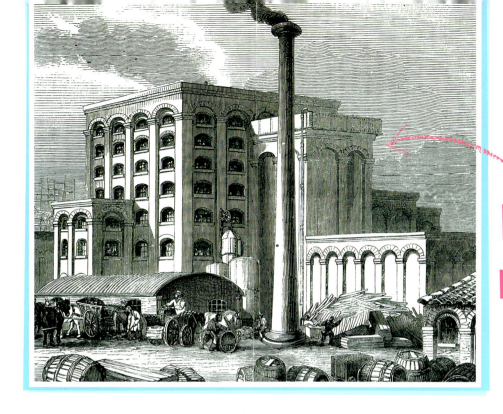

BRITAIN RESISTS

The end of the slave trade helped the sugar beet industry in Britain. This pushed up the cost of making cane sugar as the plantation owners now had to pay their labourers. By 1880, beet had replaced cane as the main source of sugar in most of Europe. Even so, the interests of British cane sugar barons stopped beet sugar being introduced into Britain. This finally changed during World War I (1914–1918), when German U-boats threatened shipping, including the ships carrying sugar. The British government responded by persuading farmers to grow sugar beet. Soon, Britain had its own thriving sugar beet industry.

SUGAR BEET IN THE USA

Many attempts were made during the 19th century to found a sugar beet industry in the USA. Perhaps the most heroic was by a missionary, John Taylor, who shipped 1,200 pounds of sugar beet seed from France to New Orleans in 1852. The seed was taken by barge and wagon up rivers and across deserts and mountain ranges to Utah.

A factory was finally built there in 1855, but because of equipment failures it never produced any sugar! The industry finally got started in 1870 when businessman Ebenezer Dyer built his factory in Alvarado, California. His success inspired others, and by 1900, 79,000 tonnes of sugar per year were being produced by 34 factories.

AN EVER SWEETER WORLD

In the 16th century, sugar was a luxury enjoyed by monarchs and wealthy nobles. Notable sugar lovers included Queen Mary of Hungary, who in 1549 hosted a ball involving sugar sculptures of deer, boar, birds and fish. Another was Elizabeth I of England, who held her own sugar banquet in 1591. She loved sugar so much that her teeth turned black.

NEW RECIPES

By the 1650s, sugar was starting to feature in the diets of the middle classes. They bought it in loaf form, ranging from the cheaper, darker Brazilian sugar to the more refined and whiter Barbadian and Jamaican varieties. Cookbooks appeared, featuring recipes for sugary desserts. One, published in 1678, included recipes for creating sugar castles, warships and forest animals. Unlike the French, who limited sugar to desserts, the English were known to mix it with meat, pies and soup dishes.

Queen Elizabeth I was famous for her sweet tooth.

TEA, COFFEE, CHOCOLATE – AND JAM

Sugar consumption rose dramatically in the 18th century, thanks to its increasing availability and the resulting drop in price.

Another reason was the growing popularity of tea, coffee and drinking chocolate, all of which became delicious when sugar was added.

The English were Europe's biggest consumers of sugar, and it was probably no coincidence that they were also its most enthusiastic tea drinkers. In 1700 the average Englishman consumed 1.8 kg of sugar a year; by 1800 he was eating 8.2 kg; and by 1900 that figure had grown to 41 kg – a massive 22-times increase in just two centuries. By this time, sugar had become a staple part of the working-class diet. Jam, for example, made of one-third fruit pulp and two-thirds sugar, was now on the breakfast table of most working-class families.

CONFECTIONARY

In the late 19th and early 20th centuries, a whole industry of sugar-based products emerged to cater for this demand for sweetness. Many of them were designed to appeal to children. These included boiled sweets, candy-floss, ice lollies, chocolate bars, caramels, fondants, fudge, toffees, liquorice, lollipops, lemon drops, marshmallows, jelly beans, bubble gum and a wide range of sugary fizzy drinks. Sugar, people discovered, combined deliciously with many different flavours and textures. It was cheap, satisfying and dangerously addictive.

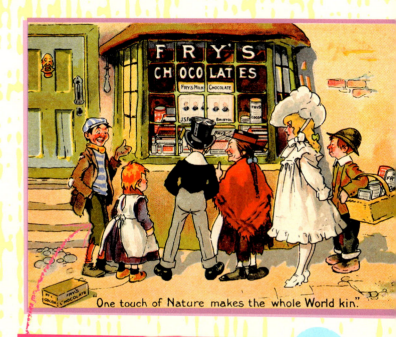

This postcard from 1908 shows children clustered around a sweet shop window.

ICE CREAM

Ice cream (12–16 per cent sugar) was first developed in Europe by the Italians in the 17th century, but remained an upper-class treat until the 19th century. The fashion for ice cream began in the USA in 1813, when it was served at the Inaugural Ball of President James Madison. By the 1850s, there were ice-cream saloons in many US cities. In 1846, one enterprising New Jersey woman, Nancy Johnson, invented a hand-cranked freezer so people could make ice cream at home. The first ice cream factory opened in Baltimore in 1851, and the 1880s saw the invention of ice cream's even more sugary cousin: the sundae.

THE CHANGING INDUSTRY

During the late 18th and 19th centuries, technology began to change the way that sugar was made. Sugar mills started to be powered by steam engines. Centrifuges were developed to separate sugar from molasses. Sugar was refined in closed vacuum pans rather than in open vessels. And in the 1830s, railroads were built to transport the sugar from factory to port. These advances began the transformation of sugar into the modern industry we know today.

THE INDUSTRY SPREADS

The 19th century also saw the spread of sugar production to other parts of the world, including Colombia, Fiji, Mauritius, Natal (South Africa) and Queensland (Australia). At that time these were all colonies of European powers with climates seen as suitable for cane sugar growth. People were shipped from other colonies to work on the plantations. They were 'indentured' labourers rather than slaves.

Indentured labourers, known insultingly as 'coolies', were people who signed a contract agreeing to work abroad for a period of five years or more. They were given a wage and a place to live, but they faced conditions that were often close to slavery. During the second half of the 19th century, the British sent 450,000 Indians as indentured labourers to the sugar plantations in the Caribbean, Natal, Mauritius and Fiji.

Forced labourers working in a sugar cane mill in the Caribbean during the 19th century.

CUBAN SUGAR

In the 1840s, Spanish-controlled Cuba emerged as the world's biggest sugar exporter. Despite pressure from Britain, the Cuban sugar planters continued to use slaves. Slavery finally ended on Cuba in 1886.

In 1898, after three brutal wars, Cuba won independence from Spain. Less than 20 per cent of its sugar mills were still functioning by this time. In this weakened state, the country's sugar industry fell under US control. The Americans built huge refineries on Cuba to process the cane, and the industry revived. By the 1950s, Cuba was exporting 5 million tonnes of sugar a year, about one-third of the world's sugar exports.

Everything changed again after a revolution on Cuba in 1959. The new leader, Fidel Castro, put the sugar industry under government control. The USA, which was buying 700,000 tonnes annually, *boycotted* Cuban sugar. The industry survived thanks to exports to its new ally, the Soviet Union, but went into steep decline in the 1990s when the Soviet Union collapsed. In 2013–14 sugar output was just 1.8 million tonnes, compared to 7.65 million tonnes in the 1980s.

A Cuban sugar plantation in about 1920. These children are sucking the juice from harvested cane.

ALVARO REYNOSO

In 1862, Cuban chemist Alvaro Reynoso published his 'Essay on the Growing of Sugarcane'. The book revolutionised the sugar industry by turning it into a science, greatly increasing the sugar yield. His proposals included recommendations on the use of fertilizers, irrigation, the ideal distance between plants and crop rotation. Reynoso helped to make Cuba the world's leading sugar producer, and the nation still celebrates 'Sugarcane Day' on Reynoso's birthday.

SUGAR TODAY

Today, sugar is produced in 121 countries around the world, and global production exceeds 170 million tonnes a year. Around 70 per cent is produced from sugarcane, and the remaining 30 per cent from sugar beet. Most sugar is consumed in the country of production, with just 25 per cent traded internationally.

NEW SWEETENERS ON THE BLOCK

The sugar industry faces competition from other sweetening products. Many consumers, worried about their weight, are turning to low-calorie or calorie-free sweeteners. These non-nutritional, man-made products can provide an intense sweet flavour and are now found in many low-calorie soft drinks and snacks.

Sugar's biggest competitor, however, is high fructose corn syrup (HFCS), produced by converting corn into the sugar fructose. This has the same flavour as sugar and is just as rich in calories, but is cheaper to produce and transport. HFCS is now found in many foods on the supermarket shelves, including soft drinks, bread, breakfast cereals, biscuits, ice cream, jam and soup.

High fructose corn syrup is now used worldwide as a sweetener.

TOP FIVE SUGAR-PRODUCING NATIONS

Annual production in metric tonnes* (2010/11)		
Brazil	38,745,000	cane
India	26,000,000	cane
China	11,475,000	beet and cane
Thailand	10,061,000	cane
USA	7,210,000	beet and cane

* 1 tonne is the equivalent of 1,000 of the normal-sized 1 kg bags of sugar you buy in the supermarket.

HEALTH ISSUES

The sugar industry continues to face anger from health campaigners who point to it as a cause of obesity. Nearly 30 per cent of the world's population is either obese or overweight, and scientific studies have shown a clear link between sugar intake and obesity.

In 2015, the World Health Organization updated its guidelines, recommending that people reduce their daily intake of sugar to less than 5 per cent (originally it was less than 10 per cent). Food producers in some countries must now include clearer labelling on products so that people know how much sugar they contain. Moves are being made to restrict advertising of sugary products to children.

A SWEET FUTURE

Sugar, which was first sipped as a juice by islanders in New Guinea thousands of years ago, is now a product enjoyed by millions of people around the world. People will always love sweet flavours, which probably means that the future of sugar is secure.

ETHANOL

The situation is not entirely bleak for sugar. Maybe, rather than eating so much of it, we can use it to power our cars! A new market is opening up that may prove to be sugar's ultimate salvation, and it's called 'ethanol'. This is a clean, affordable, low-carbon transport fuel, and it can be produced by *fermenting* sugarcane juice and molasses. Brazil is currently the world leader in the production of sugarcane ethanol. Today, 42 per cent of Brazilian transport fuel comes from this source.

TIMELINE

c. 9000 BCE	Sugarcane is first grown on New Guinea.
c. 1000	Sugarcane cultivation reaches India.
510	Darius, the Persian emperor, invades India and the Persians learn about sugar.
c. 500	Indian manufacturers start to make cooled sugar syrup, moulded in large flat bowls for easy transport.
c. 400–300	Indian manufacturers learn to convert cane juice into granulated sugar crystals.
327	Alexander the Great invades Persia and the Greeks learn about sugar.
c. 200	The Chinese learn about sugar manufacture.
CE 642	The Arabs invade Persia and discover sugarcane and sugar production techniques.
1100–1200	Sugar is rediscovered by Europeans during the Crusades.
1400s	Sugar is refined in Venice.
1493	Christopher Columbus plants sugarcane in the New World.
1509	The first sugarcane plantation is founded in the New World, on Jamaica.
1747	Andreas Marggraf discovers a method of extracting sugar crystals from beets.
1750	By this date there are 120 sugar refineries in Britain, producing a total of 30,000 tonnes of sugar per year.
1794	Slavery is abolished in the French sugar colonies.
1802	Franz Achard establishes the world's first beet sugar factory.
1807	Britain abolishes the slave trade.
1813	British chemist Edward Charles Howard invents a quicker and easier method of refining sugar.
1852	David Weston is the first to use a centrifuge to separate sugar from molasses.
1862	Alvaro Reynoso's 'Essay on the Growing of Sugarcane' helps to give a scientific basis to sugarcane cultivation.
1874	The British government abolishes the sugar tax, bringing prices down to make it more affordable for ordinary people.
1879	Russian Chemist Constantine Fahlberg accidentally discovers saccharin, the first artificial sweetener.
1920s	Brazil starts producing ethanol from sugarcane to fuel its cars.
1957	Richard Marshall and Earl Kool develop high fructose corn syrup (HFCS).
2015	The World Health Organization recommends that people reduce their daily intake of sugar to less than 5 per cent.

GLOSSARY

bacteria Tiny living things that can benefit our health, but can also cause disease.

biofuel Fuel that comes from living things that can be regrown or remade.

boycott To not use or buy products or services to show support for a cause.

calorie A unit of energy gained from food.

carbohydrate A substance found in food that gives energy to animals.

carbon dioxide A colourless, odourless gas.

centrifuge A machine designed to rapidly spin fluids to separate liquids from solids.

colony A country controlled by another country.

crystal A see-through solid where the atoms or molecules are arranged in a repeating pattern.

distillery Where alcoholic drinks are made.

evaporate To turn from liquid into gas.

export To send goods abroad to sell them.

fermenting (of a substance) Breaking down a substance with chemicals, such as bacteria.

fossil fuel Fuel made from plant or animal remains over millions of years, such as coal or oil.

fructose A simple type of sugar, found in honey, fruits, flowers, berries and most root vegetables.

glucose A sugar that is found in fruit and honey, and is a key source of energy for humans.

import To bring goods into a country from abroad to sell them.

irrigation A system used to water crops.

lactose A sugar found in milk and dairy products.

maltose The sugar produced when starch is broken down.

membrane A tiny, thin wall that acts as a boundary or lining around a cell or organ.

microorganisms Tiny living things, such as a bacterium, virus or fungus.

molasses Thick, dark brown juice that is a leftover product from raw sugar.

New World Used by Europeans to describe the Americas after it was first visited by explorers.

starch A white and tasteless substance found in foods such as potatoes, rice, bread and pasta.

sucrose The scientific name for table sugar.

turbine A machine for producing power by the fast-moving flow of water, steam, gas, air or other fluids turning a wheel or rotor.

type 2 diabetes A disorder that happens when the body can't lower sugar levels properly.

FURTHER INFORMATION

Books

Biography of Sugar (How Did That Get There?) by Rachel Eagen (CRABTREE, 2006)

Sugar (World Commodities) by Garry Chapman and Gary Hodges (SMART APPLE MEDIA, 2010)

Sugar by Jewel Parker Rhodes (LITTLE, BROWN, 2014) – a story about life on a sugar plantation

Sugar Changed the World: A Story of Magic, Spice, Slavery, Freedom and Science by Marc Aronson and Marina Budhos (CLARION BOOKS, 2010)

Sweet: The Highs and Lows of Sugar by Jennifer Greenwald (LOTUS IN BLOOM, 2014)

Websites

www.bbcgoodfood.com/howto/guide/truth-about-sugar

www.exploratorium.edu/cooking/candy/sugar.html

ngm.nationalgeographic.com/2013/08/sugar/cohen-text

www.sucrose.com/learn.html

www.sugarnutrition.org.uk/

INDEX

THE STORY OF FOOD

TITLES IN THE SERIES

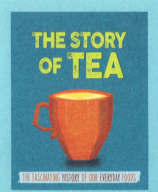

What is Tea?
The Production Process
The Birth of Tea
The Japanese Tea Ceremony
Tea Comes to Europe
Is Tea Healthy?
The Tea Trade
Taxes and Smuggling
The Boston Tea Party
Customs and Rituals
Tea Clippers
The Tea Bag
The Modern World

ISBN: 9780750296618

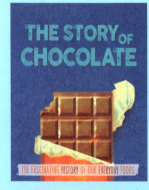

What is Chocolate?
Cacao Farming
From Beans to Chocolate
The Origins of Chocolate
The Spanish Discover
    Chocolate
Chocolate and Health
Chocolate Comes to Europe
The Plantations
The Birth of an Industry
The Arrival of the
    Chocolate Bar
Swiss Chocolate
The Henry Ford of
    Chocolate Makers
Chocolate Today

ISBN: 9780750296595

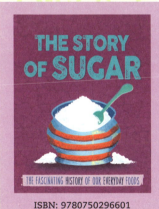

What is Sugar?
How is Sugar Used?
Sugarcane
Sugar Beet
Ancient Times
Sugar and Our Health
The Middle Ages
Sugarcane and the Americas
Sugar and Slavery
Sugar Beet in Europe
An Ever Sweeter World
The Changing Industry
Sugar Today

ISBN: 9780750296601

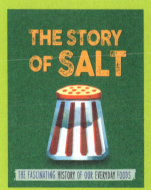

What is Salt?
Salt for Seasoning
How is Salt Produced?
Salt for Preserving Food
Salt in the Ancient World
Salt and Our Health
Salt in Religion
Salt in the Middle Ages
Exploring the New World
Salt Wars
Salt in Early America
The Salt March
Salt in Today's World

ISBN: 9780750296588

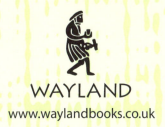

WAYLAND
www.waylandbooks.co.uk